Copyright © 2023 by Herman Strange (Author)

All rights reserved. This book or any portion thereof may not be reproduced or used in any manner whatsoever without the express written permission of the publisher except for the use of brief quotations in a book review.

This book is copyright protected. This is only for personal use. You cannot amend, distributor, sell, use, quote or paraphrase any part or the content within this book without the consent of the author. Please note the information contained within this document is for educational and entertainment purposes only. Every attempt has been made to provide accurate, up to date and reliable complete information. No warranties of any kind are expressed or implied.

Readers acknowledge that the author is not engaging in the rendering of legal, financial, medical or professional advice. The content of this book has been derived from various sources. Please consult a licensed professional before attempting any techniques outlined in this book.

By reading this document, the readers agree that under no circumstances are the author responsible for any losses, direct or indirect, which are incurred as a result of the use of information contained within this document, including but not limited to errors, omissions or inaccuracies.

Thank you very much for reading this book.

Beyond the Coin: The Untold Stories of Altcoins and Their Impact on the Crypto Landscape
Subtitle: The Rise, Fall, and Evolution of Cryptocurrencies

Series: Blockchain and Cryptocurrency Exposed
Author: Herman Strange

Table of Contents

Introduction 5
   Explanation of Altcoins and their relation to Bitcoin 5
   Purpose of the book and what it aims to cover 8
   Brief history of Altcoins and their impact on the crypto landscape 10

Chapter 1: The Pioneers 13
   Introduction of the pioneers of altcoins 13
   Their reasons for developing an alternative to Bitcoin .. 15
   Description of the first altcoins to emerge 18
   Analysis of the initial impact of altcoins on the crypto industry 21

Chapter 2: The Rise of Altcoins 24
   Overview of the rise of altcoins 24
   Emergence of new altcoins and their unique features 26
   The rise of the initial batch of altcoins 29
   Examination of the reasons for the growth of altcoins ... 31

Chapter 3: The Fall of Altcoins 33
   Explanation of why some altcoins failed 33
   Analysis of the factors that contributed to their fall 36
   Descriptions of significant altcoin crashes 39
   Lessons learned from the fall of altcoins 44

Chapter 4: The Evolution of Altcoins 47
   Explanation of how altcoins have evolved 47
   The emergence of new types of altcoins 53
   The impact of altcoins on the broader crypto ecosystem 56

Examination of the role of altcoins in the future of cryptocurrency 59

Chapter 5: Altcoins Today 62
Overview of the current state of altcoins 62
Examination of significant altcoins today 65
Exploration of the future of altcoins 71

Chapter 6: Altcoins vs Bitcoin 74
Comparison of altcoins and Bitcoin 74
Advantages and disadvantages of each 77
Examination of the relationship between altcoins and Bitcoin 80
Analysis of the potential future impact of altcoins and Bitcoin 84

Conclusion 90
Recap of the impact of altcoins on the crypto industry .. 90
Reflection on the lessons learned from the rise and fall of altcoins 93
Examination of the potential future of altcoins 96
Final thoughts on the role of altcoins in the future of cryptocurrency 99

Potential References 102

Introduction
Explanation of Altcoins and their relation to Bitcoin

Cryptocurrency is a digital or virtual form of currency that operates independently of any central bank or financial institution. Bitcoin is the first and most well-known cryptocurrency, which was introduced in 2009 by an anonymous person or group of people under the pseudonym Satoshi Nakamoto. Bitcoin operates on a decentralized ledger called the blockchain, which records all transactions in a transparent and immutable manner.

Altcoins, or alternative cryptocurrencies, are any digital assets that operate in a similar manner to Bitcoin, but with some variations in their technical design, governance, and purpose. Altcoins can be seen as an alternative to Bitcoin, providing different features, advantages, and use cases that are not available on Bitcoin. While Bitcoin remains the dominant cryptocurrency in terms of market capitalization, trading volume, and public awareness, there are thousands of altcoins that have emerged since the early days of Bitcoin, each with its own community, technology, and vision.

The relation between Bitcoin and altcoins can be seen from two perspectives: technical and conceptual. From a technical standpoint, altcoins are based on the same underlying technology as Bitcoin, which is the blockchain. However, altcoins may use different consensus algorithms, mining methods, block sizes, transaction speeds, or privacy features compared to Bitcoin. For example, some altcoins use proof-of-stake instead of proof-of-work to validate transactions, or they may have faster block times and lower fees than Bitcoin.

From a conceptual standpoint, altcoins represent a diverse range of ideas, philosophies, and visions that go beyond Bitcoin's original purpose as a peer-to-peer electronic cash system. Altcoins may aim to solve different problems, such as scalability, interoperability, privacy, governance, or social impact. Altcoins may also have different target audiences, such as investors, developers, gamers, or social activists. Altcoins may also have different forms of governance, such as decentralized autonomous organizations (DAOs) or community-driven initiatives.

Despite their differences, altcoins and Bitcoin share some common characteristics and challenges. Altcoins rely on the same network effects, user adoption, and infrastructure as Bitcoin, which means that they are subject to the same market forces, regulatory issues, and technical limitations. Altcoins also face the challenge of standing out from the crowd and building a strong community, especially in a highly competitive and rapidly evolving market. Altcoins may also be affected by Bitcoin's dominance and influence, which can either benefit or harm their reputation, adoption, and innovation.

In summary, altcoins are alternative cryptocurrencies that operate in a similar manner to Bitcoin, but with different technical and conceptual features. Altcoins represent a diverse and evolving landscape of innovation and experimentation in the crypto industry, offering different use cases, advantages, and challenges compared to Bitcoin. Understanding the relation between Bitcoin and altcoins is crucial for anyone who wants to navigate the complex and dynamic world of cryptocurrency.

Purpose of the book and what it aims to cover

The purpose of this book is to provide readers with a comprehensive understanding of altcoins, their history, and their impact on the cryptocurrency landscape. By examining the pioneers, rise, fall, and evolution of altcoins, readers will gain insight into how these digital assets have shaped the crypto industry and what their potential future may hold.

The book aims to cover a broad range of topics related to altcoins, from their emergence as an alternative to Bitcoin to their current state and potential future. By providing an in-depth analysis of the pioneers of altcoins, readers will understand the motivations and vision behind the development of these digital assets. The book will also explore the unique features and characteristics of altcoins and how they have contributed to their growth and impact on the crypto industry.

Additionally, the book will examine the challenges and obstacles that have faced altcoins, resulting in the fall of many projects. By learning from these lessons, readers will gain valuable insights into the potential risks and pitfalls that come with investing in altcoins.

The book will also explore the evolution of altcoins and the emergence of new types of digital assets, such as stablecoins and security tokens. By examining the impact of altcoins on the broader crypto ecosystem, readers will understand the role of altcoins in the future of cryptocurrency.

Furthermore, the book will provide a detailed overview of the current state of altcoins and significant projects that have gained traction in recent years. By analyzing the impact of altcoins on the crypto industry, readers will understand the potential benefits and drawbacks of investing in these digital assets.

Lastly, the book will compare altcoins to Bitcoin and examine their advantages and disadvantages. By exploring the relationship between altcoins and Bitcoin, readers will gain a deeper understanding of the potential future impact of these digital assets on the cryptocurrency landscape.

Overall, the book aims to provide readers with a comprehensive understanding of altcoins and their impact on the crypto industry. By examining the pioneers, rise, fall, and evolution of altcoins, readers will gain valuable insights into the potential future of these digital assets and the role they may play in the future of cryptocurrency.

Brief history of Altcoins and their impact on the crypto landscape

Altcoins, or alternative cryptocurrencies, have played a significant role in the development of the crypto landscape since their emergence in 2011. To understand their impact on the industry today, it's important to look back at their history and how they have evolved over time.

The first altcoin, Namecoin, was launched in 2011 as a fork of Bitcoin. It was designed to create a decentralized domain name system that was resistant to censorship and government control. Namecoin's development sparked interest in the idea of creating alternative cryptocurrencies that could offer different features and use cases from Bitcoin.

In the following years, many other altcoins emerged, each with their own unique features and goals. Litecoin, launched in 2011, was one of the first altcoins to gain significant traction. It was designed to be a faster and more efficient version of Bitcoin, with a faster block time and a different mining algorithm.

Other notable altcoins that emerged in the early days of the industry include Ripple, which was designed to facilitate cross-border payments, and Ethereum, which introduced smart contracts and decentralized applications to the blockchain.

Altcoins began to gain popularity as investors and traders sought to diversify their holdings and find new investment opportunities. As the number of altcoins grew, so did the complexity of the crypto landscape. Trading platforms and exchanges emerged to support the buying and selling of altcoins, and the industry began to take shape as a new asset class.

The impact of altcoins on the crypto landscape has been significant. They have provided users with more options and use cases than Bitcoin alone, and have driven innovation in the industry. They have also created a more diverse and competitive market, with new projects emerging all the time.

However, the rise of altcoins has not been without challenges. Many altcoins have failed to gain traction or have been plagued by issues such as security vulnerabilities, scams, and lack of liquidity. Some have even been accused of being outright scams, with developers disappearing after raising funds through initial coin offerings (ICOs).

Despite these challenges, altcoins remain a crucial part of the crypto landscape. They continue to drive innovation and provide users with new options and opportunities. As the industry continues to evolve, it will be interesting to see how altcoins continue to shape the future of cryptocurrency.

Chapter 1: The Pioneers

Introduction of the pioneers of altcoins

Bitcoin was the first decentralized cryptocurrency and was designed to offer an alternative to traditional currency systems. However, some people in the early crypto community felt that Bitcoin had limitations and believed that there was room for other cryptocurrencies with different features and use cases. This led to the emergence of altcoins or alternative cryptocurrencies.

The pioneers of altcoins were those who first recognized the potential of cryptocurrencies and sought to create new coins with different characteristics than Bitcoin. These early pioneers were instrumental in the creation of the cryptocurrency ecosystem we know today.

One of the earliest and most well-known pioneers of altcoins is Charlie Lee, who created Litecoin in 2011. Lee was an early Bitcoin adopter and saw the potential for a faster and more scalable cryptocurrency. Litecoin was designed to be four times faster than Bitcoin, with a total supply of 84 million coins compared to Bitcoin's 21 million.

Another pioneer of altcoins is Jackson Palmer, who created Dogecoin in 2013. Dogecoin was initially created as a joke, inspired by the popular "Doge" meme, but quickly gained a loyal following. Palmer's vision for Dogecoin was to create a fun and accessible cryptocurrency that could reach a wider audience than Bitcoin.

Another significant pioneer of altcoins is Vitalik Buterin, who created Ethereum in 2015. Ethereum was designed to be more than just a cryptocurrency - it was meant to be a platform for creating decentralized applications (dApps) that could run on its blockchain. Ethereum introduced the concept of smart contracts, which allowed developers to create complex applications with self-executing code.

Other early pioneers of altcoins include Namecoin, Peercoin, and Feathercoin, all of which were created in the early days of cryptocurrency. These early altcoins paved the way for a new generation of cryptocurrencies that would go on to have a significant impact on the crypto landscape.

The pioneers of altcoins were motivated by different factors, but they all shared a desire to create something new and innovative. Some wanted to improve upon Bitcoin's limitations, while others saw an opportunity to create a cryptocurrency with a unique use case. Regardless of their motivations, the pioneers of altcoins played a critical role in the evolution of cryptocurrency and helped to create a vibrant and diverse ecosystem of digital assets.

Their reasons for developing an alternative to Bitcoin

The pioneers of altcoins had various reasons for developing an alternative to Bitcoin. Some of these reasons were technical in nature, while others were philosophical or ideological. In this section, we will explore some of the key reasons why the pioneers of altcoins felt the need to create alternatives to Bitcoin.

Limitations of Bitcoin

One of the main reasons why the pioneers of altcoins felt the need to create alternatives to Bitcoin was due to its limitations. While Bitcoin was the first cryptocurrency and had a significant impact on the financial industry, it had several limitations. These limitations included slow transaction times, high fees, and a limited block size, which made it difficult to scale. Some of the pioneers of altcoins felt that these limitations could be overcome by creating new cryptocurrencies with improved technical specifications.

Philosophical differences

Another reason why the pioneers of altcoins developed alternative cryptocurrencies was due to philosophical differences with Bitcoin. While Bitcoin was designed to be decentralized and free from government control, some of the pioneers of altcoins felt that it did not go far enough in terms of privacy and anonymity. They believed that cryptocurrencies could be used to create a more private and anonymous financial system that would be resistant to government interference.

Experimentation

Another reason why the pioneers of altcoins created alternative cryptocurrencies was simply for experimentation. Many of these individuals were computer programmers and technology enthusiasts who wanted to experiment with creating their own cryptocurrencies. They saw Bitcoin as a starting point and wanted to explore the possibilities of creating new cryptocurrencies with different features and technical specifications.

Market demand

Finally, some of the pioneers of altcoins created their own cryptocurrencies in response to market demand. As more people became interested in cryptocurrency, they began to realize that Bitcoin had limitations and that there was room for other cryptocurrencies with different features and use cases. Some of the pioneers of altcoins saw an opportunity to create cryptocurrencies that could address specific market niches and meet the needs of different types of users.

Overall, the pioneers of altcoins had a variety of reasons for developing alternatives to Bitcoin. Some of these reasons were technical in nature, while others were ideological or driven by market demand. Despite their differences, the pioneers of altcoins shared a common goal of creating new and innovative cryptocurrencies that could have a positive impact on the financial industry.

Description of the first altcoins to emerge

In the early days of cryptocurrency, Bitcoin was the only game in town. However, it didn't take long for other developers to recognize the potential of blockchain technology and begin to create their own digital currencies. These early alternative coins, or altcoins, were primarily created to address perceived shortcomings in Bitcoin, such as slow transaction processing times, high fees, and limited functionality.

The first altcoin to emerge was Namecoin, which was created in 2011 by an anonymous developer known only by the pseudonym "Vinced." Namecoin was designed to be a decentralized domain name system, allowing users to register and manage domain names without the need for a central authority. It was also the first altcoin to use a merged mining protocol, which allowed miners to simultaneously mine Namecoin and Bitcoin without any loss of hashing power.

Another early altcoin was Litecoin, which was launched in 2011 by former Google engineer Charlie Lee. Litecoin was designed to address some of the issues with Bitcoin, such as slow transaction processing times and high fees. It used a different hashing algorithm than Bitcoin, which made it resistant to ASIC mining and more accessible to ordinary users with regular computer hardware.

In 2012, the Ripple payment protocol and the associated XRP digital currency were launched by OpenCoin, a company co-founded by Chris Larsen and Jed McCaleb. Ripple was designed to facilitate fast and cheap cross-border payments, making it a potential competitor to traditional payment systems like SWIFT. Unlike Bitcoin and most other cryptocurrencies, XRP is not mined, but instead uses a consensus algorithm to validate transactions.

Another notable altcoin from the early days of cryptocurrency was Peercoin, which was launched in 2012 by software developer Sunny King. Peercoin was designed to address some of the environmental concerns associated with Bitcoin mining, which requires a huge amount of energy. Peercoin introduced a hybrid proof-of-stake and proof-of-work consensus algorithm, which allowed users to mine new coins by holding existing coins in a wallet.

In addition to these early altcoins, there were many others that emerged in the years following Bitcoin's launch. Some were designed to address specific use cases, such as Dogecoin, which was created as a humorous tribute to the Shiba Inu dog meme and quickly became popular as a tipping currency on social media platforms. Others, like

Feathercoin and Novacoin, were created as direct competitors to Bitcoin, but ultimately failed to gain traction.

Despite the fact that many of these early altcoins were not successful in the long run, they played an important role in the evolution of the cryptocurrency landscape. They introduced new ideas, features, and use cases, and provided valuable lessons for future projects to learn from. Without these early pioneers, the crypto industry would not be what it is today.

Analysis of the initial impact of altcoins on the crypto industry

The introduction of altcoins had a profound impact on the crypto industry, and this impact was felt almost immediately. When the first altcoins were introduced, they were met with a mix of excitement and skepticism. Some saw them as an opportunity to improve upon Bitcoin's shortcomings, while others viewed them as unnecessary distractions that would only dilute the crypto ecosystem.

Despite this initial uncertainty, altcoins quickly began to gain traction, and their impact on the crypto industry was undeniable. In this section, we will analyze the initial impact of altcoins on the crypto industry.

One of the most significant impacts of altcoins was their role in increasing public awareness of cryptocurrencies. Bitcoin had already gained a degree of mainstream attention, but the introduction of altcoins brought further attention to the crypto industry. This increased awareness brought more investors and enthusiasts into the space, which contributed to the growth of the crypto market as a whole.

Altcoins also helped to address some of the concerns that people had with Bitcoin. One of the most significant concerns was scalability. Bitcoin's block size limit was seen as a bottleneck that would limit its ability to handle a large number of transactions. Altcoins like Litecoin and Bitcoin Cash, which had larger block sizes, offered a potential solution to this problem. By addressing this scalability issue, altcoins provided a way to demonstrate that cryptocurrencies could be viable alternatives to traditional payment methods.

Another significant impact of altcoins was their role in pushing the boundaries of what was possible with cryptocurrencies. Altcoins introduced new features and use cases that were not possible with Bitcoin. For example, Namecoin introduced the concept of a decentralized domain name system, while Ethereum introduced the concept of smart contracts. These innovations helped to showcase the potential of blockchain technology beyond just a payment system.

In addition, altcoins also helped to promote healthy competition within the crypto industry. Bitcoin was no longer the only game in town, and this competition encouraged developers to innovate and improve upon existing technology. This competition also helped to drive down costs, as exchanges and other service providers had to compete with each other to attract users.

However, the initial impact of altcoins was not all positive. The introduction of new cryptocurrencies created confusion among investors and made it more difficult to differentiate between legitimate projects and scams. Additionally, the rapid proliferation of altcoins created a fragmented market that made it more difficult for investors to track their investments.

Despite these challenges, the initial impact of altcoins was overwhelmingly positive. They brought new ideas and innovations to the crypto industry and helped to demonstrate the potential of blockchain technology beyond just a payment system. They also helped to increase public awareness of cryptocurrencies and encouraged healthy competition within the industry.

Chapter 2: The Rise of Altcoins
Overview of the rise of altcoins

The rise of altcoins marked a significant moment in the history of cryptocurrency. While Bitcoin had paved the way for digital currencies, it wasn't long before other projects emerged seeking to capitalize on the new technology.

The first wave of altcoins began to emerge in 2011, with projects like Namecoin and Litecoin introducing new features and innovations. Over time, new altcoins continued to appear, with each project attempting to carve out a unique niche in the market.

As more altcoins appeared, they began to garner more attention from investors and traders. This led to a surge in demand for altcoins and a rapid increase in their value. In some cases, altcoins outperformed Bitcoin, making them an attractive investment option for those seeking to diversify their cryptocurrency holdings.

One of the factors driving the rise of altcoins was their ability to address some of the shortcomings of Bitcoin. While Bitcoin was seen as a revolutionary new technology, it still had some limitations. For example, Bitcoin's transaction processing time was slow, and its transaction fees were relatively high. Altcoins were able to address these issues by introducing new technologies and features that made them faster and cheaper to use.

Another key factor in the rise of altcoins was the growing interest in blockchain technology. As more people began to understand the potential of blockchain, they became more interested in investing in projects that were leveraging this technology. Altcoins offered a way for investors to participate in the blockchain revolution and potentially profit from its growth.

Overall, the rise of altcoins was driven by a combination of factors, including their ability to address some of the shortcomings of Bitcoin, their potential for innovation, and growing interest in blockchain technology. As the number of altcoins continued to grow, the crypto landscape became increasingly diverse, opening up new opportunities and challenges for investors and traders.

Emergence of new altcoins and their unique features

As the popularity of Bitcoin continued to grow, developers and enthusiasts began to explore alternative cryptocurrencies that could address some of Bitcoin's limitations and provide unique features and benefits. This led to the emergence of numerous altcoins with different approaches, goals, and features. In this section, we'll explore some of the most prominent altcoins that have emerged since the early days of cryptocurrency.

Litecoin: One of the earliest and most successful altcoins, Litecoin was created in 2011 by Charlie Lee, a former Google engineer. Lee designed Litecoin to be a "lite" version of Bitcoin, with faster transaction times and lower fees. Litecoin uses a different algorithm for mining than Bitcoin, which allows for more efficient use of computer resources and a greater degree of decentralization.

Ethereum: Launched in 2015 by Vitalik Buterin, Ethereum is more than just a cryptocurrency. It's a platform that allows developers to create decentralized applications (dapps) using smart contracts. Smart contracts are self-executing programs that run on the Ethereum blockchain and can automate various types of transactions and agreements. Ethereum has been a game-changer in the crypto industry, enabling the creation of new types of applications and services that were previously impossible.

Ripple: Ripple is a cryptocurrency that was created in 2012 by Ripple Labs. Unlike most cryptocurrencies, Ripple is not based on blockchain technology. Instead, it uses a unique consensus algorithm to validate transactions, which allows for faster and more efficient processing. Ripple is primarily designed for use in international money transfers, with the goal of reducing the time and cost of cross-border payments.

Monero: Monero is a privacy-focused cryptocurrency that was launched in 2014. It uses a unique privacy protocol that obscures the sender, receiver, and amount of every transaction on the network. This makes Monero transactions virtually untraceable and anonymous. Monero has become popular among individuals who value privacy and security, including those involved in illegal activities.

Dogecoin: Created in 2013 by Billy Markus and Jackson Palmer as a joke based on the "Doge" internet meme, Dogecoin has become a cult favorite among cryptocurrency enthusiasts. Despite its origins as a parody, Dogecoin has developed a loyal following and has been used for various charitable causes and community-driven initiatives. Dogecoin's popularity surged in 2021, driven in part by social media hype and celebrity endorsements.

These are just a few examples of the many altcoins that have emerged over the years. Each altcoin has its own unique features and goals, and some have been more successful than others. However, the rise of altcoins has shown that there is significant demand for alternatives to Bitcoin and that the crypto industry is constantly evolving and expanding.

The rise of the initial batch of altcoins

As the first batch of altcoins gained popularity and success, other developers began creating their own alternative coins, leading to a rapid proliferation of altcoins. The initial batch of altcoins included Litecoin, Namecoin, and Peercoin.

Litecoin was launched in October 2011 by Charlie Lee, a former Google engineer. Lee designed Litecoin to address some of the limitations of Bitcoin, such as slower transaction times and higher fees. Litecoin uses a different hashing algorithm than Bitcoin, called Scrypt, which is designed to be more memory-intensive and resistant to ASIC mining.

Namecoin was launched in April 2011 by a developer known as "Vinced" on the Bitcointalk forum. Namecoin was the first altcoin to use a decentralized naming system, allowing users to register and store domain names on the blockchain. This made Namecoin a pioneer in the concept of using the blockchain for more than just financial transactions.

Peercoin was launched in August 2012 by Sunny King and Scott Nadal. Peercoin introduced a new consensus mechanism called Proof-of-Stake (PoS), which aims to address some of the energy consumption and centralization issues associated with Bitcoin's Proof-of-Work (PoW) mechanism. In PoS, instead of miners competing to solve complex mathematical puzzles to validate transactions, validators are chosen based on the number of coins they hold and are willing to "stake" or lock up as collateral.

These initial altcoins each brought their own unique features and innovations to the crypto landscape, and were able to attract a dedicated community of users and developers. Their success helped pave the way for the rise of other altcoins with their own unique features and use cases.

Examination of the reasons for the growth of altcoins

Altcoins have grown in popularity and market capitalization over the years, with some even surpassing Bitcoin in market value. There are several reasons for this growth, including:

Innovation and unique features: Many altcoins were developed with unique features that distinguished them from Bitcoin. For example, Litecoin was designed to offer faster transaction times than Bitcoin, while Ripple was designed to facilitate fast and low-cost cross-border payments. These unique features and innovations have made some altcoins more appealing to investors and users than Bitcoin.

Diversification: As the crypto market grew, investors began to diversify their portfolios beyond Bitcoin, seeking out altcoins that they believed had strong potential. This has led to increased demand for altcoins and has contributed to their growth.

Speculation and hype: Like any asset, altcoins have been subject to speculation and hype, with some investors and traders buying into altcoins based on rumors or hearsay. This has led to price bubbles in some altcoins, with prices rising quickly before crashing back down.

Accessibility and ease of use: As the crypto industry has matured, it has become easier for investors and users to access and use altcoins. Many exchanges now allow users to buy and trade altcoins alongside Bitcoin, and there are numerous wallets and apps that support a range of altcoins.

Community support: Altcoins often have strong communities of developers, enthusiasts, and supporters who are passionate about the project and are willing to invest time and resources into its growth. This support can lead to increased adoption and usage of the altcoin.

Overall, the growth of altcoins can be attributed to a combination of factors, including innovation, diversification, speculation, accessibility, and community support. As the crypto market continues to evolve, it remains to be seen which altcoins will continue to thrive and which will fall by the wayside.

Chapter 3: The Fall of Altcoins

Explanation of why some altcoins failed

Despite the excitement and potential surrounding the rise of altcoins, not all projects were successful. In fact, many altcoins have failed to gain traction and have ultimately been abandoned or delisted from exchanges. There are a variety of reasons why an altcoin may fail, including poor execution, lack of community support, regulatory issues, or market volatility. In this section, we will explore some of the common reasons why altcoins fail and examine specific examples of failed altcoin projects.

One of the most common reasons for altcoin failure is poor execution. Altcoin development requires significant technical expertise and resources, and not all projects are able to deliver on their promises. This can include issues with the development team, such as lack of experience or poor communication, or problems with the underlying technology itself. In some cases, the technology may be promising in theory but difficult to implement in practice, leading to delays, bugs, or other issues.

Another factor that can contribute to altcoin failure is lack of community support. Unlike Bitcoin, which has a large and passionate community of supporters, many altcoins struggle to attract a dedicated following. This can be due to a variety of factors, such as poor marketing, lack of transparency, or a failure to deliver on promised features. Without a strong community to advocate for the project, it can be difficult for an altcoin to gain traction and build momentum.

Regulatory issues are another potential obstacle for altcoins. While Bitcoin and other cryptocurrencies exist outside of traditional financial systems, they are still subject to a variety of laws and regulations. Altcoins that fail to comply with regulatory requirements may face legal action or be forced to shut down entirely. In some cases, the threat of regulatory action can deter investors or community members from supporting an altcoin project.

Market volatility is another risk for altcoins, particularly those that are relatively new or unproven. The cryptocurrency market is notoriously volatile, with prices fluctuating rapidly in response to a variety of factors. Altcoins that are unable to weather these fluctuations may see their value drop precipitously, potentially leading to investor panic or a loss of confidence in the project.

Specific examples of failed altcoins include projects like Paycoin, which promised to be a "Bitcoin killer" but ultimately collapsed amid allegations of fraud and market manipulation. Other examples include BitConnect, which was accused of operating a Ponzi scheme, and Moolah, which raised millions of dollars through an initial coin offering (ICO) but ultimately failed to deliver on its promises.

Overall, the failure of altcoins highlights the challenges and risks inherent in the cryptocurrency space. While some projects have been successful, others have struggled to gain traction or have been outright scams. As the crypto industry continues to evolve, it will be important for investors and developers to learn from these failures and work to create sustainable, reliable altcoin projects that can make a positive impact on the crypto landscape.

Analysis of the factors that contributed to their fall

The fall of altcoins is a complex issue, and there are various factors that contributed to their demise. Understanding these factors is crucial for preventing similar failures in the future and ensuring the sustainability of the cryptocurrency market. In this section, we will examine some of the significant reasons why altcoins failed and the factors that contributed to their downfall.

Lack of Adoption:

One of the primary reasons why some altcoins failed was the lack of adoption. Cryptocurrencies need to have widespread adoption to be successful, but many altcoins failed to achieve this. Many altcoins failed to gain traction among users and businesses, leading to low trading volumes and low demand. This lack of adoption was often due to a lack of understanding of the altcoin's value proposition, poor marketing, or a lack of development resources.

Scams and Fraud:

The cryptocurrency market is notorious for its scams and fraudulent activities, and many altcoins fell victim to these scams. Some developers created altcoins with no real purpose or value, and they used deceptive marketing tactics to promote them. These scams often took advantage of new or inexperienced investors, promising them huge returns on their investments.

Poor Security:

Another significant factor that contributed to the downfall of some altcoins was poor security. Many altcoins were vulnerable to hacking attacks or other security breaches, leading to loss of user funds and a loss of trust in the altcoin. Some altcoins were also susceptible to 51% attacks, where a group of miners could take control of the network and manipulate transactions.

Lack of Innovation:

The cryptocurrency market is highly competitive, and altcoins need to provide innovative solutions to be successful. However, some altcoins failed to innovate, and they were unable to offer anything new or unique to users. These altcoins were often just copies of existing cryptocurrencies, lacking any real value proposition.

Lack of Community Support:

Community support is essential for the success of any cryptocurrency, and many altcoins failed to garner enough support from their communities. A lack of community support often leads to low trading volumes and little interest in the altcoin. Community support is also crucial for the development and growth of the altcoin, as developers need feedback and support from the community to improve the technology.

Market Volatility:

Cryptocurrencies are known for their volatility, and this can be particularly challenging for altcoins. Altcoins are often more susceptible to market fluctuations than established cryptocurrencies, and this volatility can lead to a loss of investor confidence and a decrease in demand.

In conclusion, the fall of altcoins was due to various factors, including lack of adoption, scams and fraud, poor security, lack of innovation, lack of community support, and market volatility. Understanding these factors is essential for preventing similar failures in the future, and it is crucial for the long-term sustainability of the cryptocurrency market.

Descriptions of significant altcoin crashes

As the crypto market grew, so did the number of altcoins available. While many altcoins have been successful, others have experienced significant crashes that have resulted in substantial losses for investors. In this section, we will explore some of the most significant altcoin crashes and the reasons behind them.

Namecoin (NMC)

Namecoin is one of the earliest altcoins to have been created. It was launched in 2011 and was designed to offer decentralized domain name registration. Namecoin was also the first altcoin to use a merged mining algorithm, allowing Bitcoin miners to mine both Namecoin and Bitcoin simultaneously. However, despite its early promise, Namecoin struggled to gain significant traction, and its value declined steadily over time. Today, Namecoin is considered a failed project, and its market capitalization is close to zero.

Feathercoin (FTC)

Feathercoin was launched in 2013 and was designed to be a lightweight version of Bitcoin. Feathercoin used a modified version of the Scrypt algorithm and promised faster transaction times and lower fees than Bitcoin. Feathercoin gained some popularity in its early days, but its value soon began to decline. In late 2013, Feathercoin experienced a significant crash, losing over 90% of its value in just a few weeks. Today, Feathercoin is considered a failed project, and its market capitalization is close to zero.

Ripple (XRP)

Ripple was launched in 2012 and was designed to offer fast and low-cost cross-border payments. Unlike most other cryptocurrencies, Ripple does not rely on mining to validate transactions. Instead, it uses a consensus algorithm that requires users to approve transactions before they can be added to the ledger. Ripple gained significant attention in 2017 and 2018, reaching a market capitalization of over $100 billion at its peak. However, in 2020, the Securities and Exchange Commission (SEC) filed a lawsuit against Ripple, alleging that XRP was an unregistered security. This lawsuit caused a significant drop in the value of XRP, and many exchanges delisted the coin. Today, XRP's market capitalization is significantly lower than its peak, and its future remains uncertain.

Bitconnect (BCC)

Bitconnect was launched in 2016 and was designed to offer a lending platform that promised high returns for investors. Bitconnect used a multi-level marketing model to attract investors, with users earning commissions for referring new users to the platform. Bitconnect's lending platform promised returns of up to 1% per day, a claim that many investors found too good to be true. In early 2018, Bitconnect was hit with cease and desist orders from several US states, and its value began to decline rapidly. In January 2018, Bitconnect shut down its lending platform, causing the value of BCC to drop over 90% in a matter of days. Today, Bitconnect is considered one of the most significant cryptocurrency scams of all time.

Mt. Gox

Mt. Gox was one of the largest cryptocurrency exchanges in the world, handling over 70% of all Bitcoin transactions at its peak. In 2014, Mt. Gox filed for bankruptcy after losing over 850,000 Bitcoins, worth over $450 million at the time. The loss of these funds was due to a hack that exploited a vulnerability in Mt. Gox's system, allowing the hackers to steal the Bitcoins. Mt. Gox's collapse was a significant blow to the cryptocurrency industry, and it caused the value of Bitcoin to drop by over 50%.

*****

One of the most significant altcoin crashes occurred in 2014 when the altcoin exchange Mt. Gox filed for bankruptcy. Mt. Gox was one of the earliest and largest Bitcoin exchanges and also allowed users to trade in other cryptocurrencies. The exchange suffered a massive hack in which 850,000 Bitcoins, worth over $450 million at the time, were stolen. This was about 7% of all Bitcoins in circulation at the time. Mt. Gox was never able to recover from the hack and ultimately filed for bankruptcy in 2014.

Another notable altcoin crash occurred in 2018, during what is known as the "crypto winter." In late 2017, the prices of many altcoins had skyrocketed to all-time highs, fueled by hype and speculation. However, the market soon entered a sharp decline, and many altcoins lost a significant amount of their value. By early 2018, many projects were struggling to keep afloat, and some ultimately failed. This period was a harsh reminder that the crypto market is still relatively new and unpredictable, and investors should exercise caution.

In 2020, the DeFi platform Yam Finance experienced a significant crash. Yam Finance had launched its token with much fanfare and gained popularity quickly due to its high returns. However, a flaw in the code was discovered that made the token vulnerable to a potential attack. The developers scrambled to fix the issue, but the damage had already been done, and the token's value plummeted by more than 99% in just a few hours.

Overall, these altcoin crashes highlight the inherent risks involved in investing in cryptocurrencies. While altcoins have the potential to generate high returns, they are also highly volatile, and investors should be prepared for the possibility of significant losses.

Lessons learned from the fall of altcoins

The rise and fall of altcoins have left valuable lessons for investors, developers, and enthusiasts in the crypto industry. Here are some of the crucial lessons learned from the fall of altcoins:

Lack of substance: Many altcoins were created with no real-world use cases, and their development was mainly fueled by hype and speculation. Investors were attracted to the potential high returns and neglected to evaluate the underlying technology and its potential for solving real-world problems.

Market saturation: The oversaturation of the market with altcoins led to increased competition and fragmentation. This made it challenging for new altcoins to gain traction and compete with established projects.

Lack of liquidity: Many altcoins lacked liquidity, making it challenging for investors to buy or sell their holdings. This led to price volatility, market manipulation, and loss of investor confidence.

Lack of regulation: The lack of regulation in the crypto industry made it easy for scammers and fraudsters to launch and promote their altcoins. This led to many investors losing their money in fraudulent schemes.

Lack of innovation: Many altcoins were mere copies of Bitcoin, with little to no innovation. The lack of innovation led to a lack of differentiation between projects, making it challenging for investors to identify promising projects.

Governance issues: Some altcoins had governance issues, making it challenging for developers to agree on important decisions affecting the project's direction. This led to community fragmentation and lack of progress in the project's development.

Security issues: Many altcoins were prone to security issues, making them vulnerable to hacks and attacks. This resulted in the loss of funds for investors and tarnished the reputation of the project.

Volatility: Altcoins are known for their high volatility, and some investors entered the market without understanding the risks involved. The high volatility resulted in many investors losing their money when the market crashed.

In conclusion, the fall of altcoins provides valuable lessons for investors, developers, and enthusiasts in the crypto industry. Investors must conduct due diligence and evaluate the underlying technology and potential real-world use cases before investing in altcoins. Developers must focus on innovation and solve real-world problems to stand out in the oversaturated market. Finally, regulators must develop a regulatory framework that protects investors from fraudulent schemes while promoting innovation in the crypto industry.

Chapter 4: The Evolution of Altcoins

Explanation of how altcoins have evolved

Since their inception, altcoins have undergone significant changes, from being simple alternatives to Bitcoin to becoming advanced blockchain networks that serve different purposes. This chapter explores how altcoins have evolved over time, the trends that have emerged, and what the future may hold.

Altcoins have come a long way since the first few were created as simple forks of the Bitcoin codebase. Over time, they have evolved to become more sophisticated, with unique features and functionalities. Some of the key ways in which altcoins have evolved include:

Diversification of use cases

The first batch of altcoins were created as a response to perceived shortcomings of Bitcoin, but they still largely served the same purpose as Bitcoin – as a digital currency. However, over time, altcoins have diversified to serve a variety of different use cases. Some altcoins, such as Litecoin and Dogecoin, still function primarily as digital currencies, while others like Ethereum and Cardano offer advanced smart contract functionalities. Other altcoins, such as Monero and Zcash, prioritize privacy and anonymity, while others like Stellar and Ripple focus on cross-border payments.

Advanced consensus mechanisms

One of the biggest criticisms of Bitcoin is its energy-intensive proof-of-work consensus mechanism. As a result, many altcoins have developed alternative consensus mechanisms to reduce energy consumption and improve scalability. For example, Ethereum uses a proof-of-stake consensus mechanism, while Ripple uses a Byzantine fault-tolerant consensus mechanism.

Integration of new technologies

Altcoins have also evolved by integrating new technologies such as zero-knowledge proofs, sharding, and sidechains. These technologies have helped to improve scalability, privacy, and security, among other things.

Governance models

As altcoins have become more complex, they have also developed new governance models to help manage their development and evolution. For example, some altcoins have implemented on-chain governance, where stakeholders can vote on proposals directly through the blockchain, while others use off-chain governance models.

Interoperability

As the number of altcoins has increased, so too has the need for interoperability between them. Some altcoins, such as Polkadot and Cosmos, have been created specifically to enable interoperability between different blockchain networks.

Trends that have emerged in altcoin development

Several trends have emerged in the development of altcoins in recent years:

Niche specialization

As the number of altcoins has grown, many have begun to specialize in specific niches. For example, there are now altcoins that focus exclusively on privacy, gaming, decentralized finance, and even art.

DeFi dominance

Decentralized finance (DeFi) has emerged as one of the most popular use cases for altcoins. Many altcoins, such as Aave and Compound, have been created specifically for DeFi applications, while others, such as Uniswap and SushiSwap, enable decentralized exchanges.

Layer 2 solutions

Scalability has been a major challenge for many blockchain networks, including altcoins. As a result, many altcoins are exploring layer 2 solutions to improve scalability. For example, Ethereum has implemented a layer

2 solution called Optimism, while other altcoins like Polygon and Arbitrum offer their own layer 2 solutions.

Environmental concerns

As the environmental impact of blockchain technology has become more widely recognized, many altcoins have begun exploring alternative consensus mechanisms that are more energy-efficient. For example, Cardano uses a proof-of-stake consensus mechanism that is significantly less energy-intensive than proof-of-work.

The Future of Altcoins

The world of cryptocurrencies is constantly evolving, and it is difficult to predict what the future holds for altcoins. However, there are several trends and developments that suggest what may be in store for these alternative digital currencies.

Increased adoption: As more people become familiar with cryptocurrencies, there is a growing interest in altcoins as an alternative to Bitcoin. This has led to an increase in adoption and use of altcoins, as people look for new investment opportunities or alternatives to traditional payment systems.

Regulation: The crypto industry is becoming increasingly regulated, with many governments implementing laws to control the use of digital currencies.

While this may present some challenges for altcoins, it could also lead to increased legitimacy and wider adoption.

Interoperability: One of the challenges of the current crypto landscape is the lack of interoperability between different blockchain platforms. However, many altcoins are working to address this issue by developing cross-chain interoperability protocols, which could lead to greater collaboration and cooperation between different cryptocurrencies.

DeFi: Decentralized finance (DeFi) is one of the most exciting developments in the crypto space, and altcoins are playing an important role in this new ecosystem. Many altcoins are being used as collateral in DeFi lending platforms or as part of decentralized exchanges (DEXs), which are becoming increasingly popular.

New use cases: As the technology behind cryptocurrencies continues to evolve, new use cases are emerging for altcoins. For example, some altcoins are being used to power decentralized applications (dApps), while others are being used for supply chain management or identity verification.

Innovation: Altcoins are known for their innovation, and this trend is likely to continue as developers come up with new and creative ways to use blockchain technology.

This could lead to new types of altcoins, as well as new applications for existing ones.

Overall, the future of altcoins is uncertain, but there are many exciting developments and possibilities on the horizon. As the crypto industry continues to mature and evolve, altcoins will likely play an important role in shaping the future of digital currencies.

The emergence of new types of altcoins

As the crypto industry continues to evolve, new types of altcoins are emerging with unique features and use cases. Some of these emerging altcoins include:

Stablecoins: These are cryptocurrencies designed to maintain a stable value, usually by pegging their value to a fiat currency like the US dollar. Stablecoins aim to address the volatility issues of other cryptocurrencies like Bitcoin and Ethereum, making them more suitable for everyday transactions.

Security Tokens: These are digital tokens that represent ownership of a real-world asset like a share in a company or real estate. Security tokens are designed to provide investors with the benefits of blockchain technology, including increased liquidity and transparency.

Utility Tokens: These are digital tokens used to access a specific service or product within a blockchain ecosystem. Utility tokens are used to incentivize users to participate in a blockchain network and provide a mechanism for value transfer within the network.

Privacy Coins: These are cryptocurrencies designed to provide users with a higher degree of anonymity and privacy in their transactions. Privacy coins use advanced cryptographic techniques to obfuscate transaction data, making it difficult to trace the sender and receiver of the transaction.

Interoperable Coins: These are cryptocurrencies designed to facilitate seamless interoperability between different blockchain networks. Interoperable coins aim to address the issue of blockchain fragmentation by providing a mechanism for cross-chain transactions.

These emerging altcoins are likely to play a significant role in the future of the crypto industry. For instance, stablecoins are increasingly being used for everyday transactions, and their market capitalization has grown significantly in recent years. As more people seek to transact using cryptocurrencies, stablecoins are likely to become even more popular.

Security tokens, on the other hand, are expected to disrupt traditional finance by providing a more efficient and transparent way to invest in real-world assets. The use of security tokens is expected to grow in the coming years, especially as regulatory frameworks are put in place to govern their issuance and trading.

Utility tokens are also expected to continue playing a significant role in the crypto industry by incentivizing users to participate in blockchain networks. As more applications are built on blockchain technology, the demand for utility tokens is likely to increase.

Privacy coins are also likely to play a crucial role in the future of the crypto industry, especially as regulators and governments seek to regulate cryptocurrencies. Privacy coins provide users with a degree of anonymity and privacy that is not possible with other cryptocurrencies, making them attractive to users who value privacy.

Interoperable coins are also expected to become more popular as blockchain networks continue to proliferate. Interoperable coins provide a mechanism for seamless value transfer between different blockchain networks, making them essential for the growth and development of the crypto industry.

Overall, the emergence of new types of altcoins is a testament to the growing maturity of the crypto industry. These emerging altcoins are likely to play a significant role in the future of the industry, providing users with new and innovative ways to transact and invest.

The impact of altcoins on the broader crypto ecosystem

The impact of altcoins on the broader crypto ecosystem has been significant, with these digital currencies offering different use cases, advantages, and drawbacks compared to Bitcoin. While Bitcoin remains the dominant cryptocurrency, altcoins have carved out a niche for themselves, and their influence on the broader crypto ecosystem is undeniable. In this section, we'll explore the impact that altcoins have had on the broader crypto ecosystem.

Increased competition and innovation Altcoins have been instrumental in increasing competition and innovation in the broader crypto ecosystem. With new altcoins emerging regularly, developers are forced to come up with innovative use cases and features to stay relevant. This has led to the creation of some of the most exciting projects in the crypto industry, such as smart contract platforms like Ethereum and Binance Smart Chain, privacy-focused coins like Monero and Zcash, and even meme-inspired coins like Dogecoin.

Diversification of the crypto portfolio Investors have also benefited from the emergence of altcoins, as they can diversify their portfolios beyond Bitcoin. Altcoins offer different risk profiles and potential returns compared to

Bitcoin, allowing investors to mitigate risk and potentially earn higher returns. Additionally, the emergence of stablecoins has made it easier for investors to hold their assets in a stable currency without having to convert back to fiat.

Decentralized finance (DeFi) Altcoins have played a significant role in the emergence of decentralized finance (DeFi), which is the concept of traditional financial services being built on blockchain technology. DeFi platforms offer a range of financial services, including borrowing and lending, staking, yield farming, and trading, among others. Many of these services are facilitated by altcoins, which serve as the native currency of these platforms.

Market volatility Altcoins have also contributed to the market volatility of the broader crypto ecosystem. The emergence of new altcoins, as well as the constant fluctuations in the value of existing altcoins, has led to increased volatility in the market. This volatility can create opportunities for traders and investors but can also be a source of risk and uncertainty.

Regulatory challenges As the number of altcoins in the market increases, regulatory challenges become more complex. Regulators are still struggling to come up with a unified approach to regulating cryptocurrencies, and the emergence of altcoins with different use cases and features makes this task even more challenging. This lack of regulatory clarity can be a significant barrier to the adoption of altcoins and can create uncertainty in the market.

Future potential The future potential of altcoins is exciting, with many projects exploring innovative use cases for blockchain technology. Altcoins like Ethereum are at the forefront of this innovation, with the platform's ability to host smart contracts and decentralized applications (dApps) opening up a range of possibilities for developers. Other altcoins, such as Polkadot and Solana, are exploring the potential of cross-chain interoperability, which could revolutionize the way different blockchains interact with each other.

Overall, the impact of altcoins on the broader crypto ecosystem has been significant, with these digital currencies driving innovation, diversification, and competition. While there have been challenges and setbacks along the way, the future potential of altcoins is vast, and they will continue to play a critical role in the development of the crypto industry.

Examination of the role of altcoins in the future of cryptocurrency

As the crypto landscape continues to evolve, the role of altcoins in the future of cryptocurrency remains an important topic of discussion. While Bitcoin remains the dominant player in the crypto space, altcoins have proven to be a vital component of the ecosystem. In this section, we will examine the potential role of altcoins in the future of cryptocurrency and the factors that may influence their success.

Adoption and integration One of the key factors that will determine the role of altcoins in the future of cryptocurrency is their adoption and integration into the broader ecosystem. As more merchants and individuals begin to accept and use altcoins for transactions, their value and utility will increase. Additionally, as altcoins become more integrated into payment systems and exchanges, they will become more accessible to a wider range of users.

Unique use cases Altcoins with unique use cases and value propositions are likely to play an increasingly important role in the future of cryptocurrency. For example, privacy-focused altcoins like Monero and Zcash have gained popularity due to their ability to offer enhanced privacy and anonymity. Similarly, altcoins like Ripple and Stellar that focus on facilitating fast and low-cost cross-border transactions are likely to play an important role in the future of international trade.

Regulation Regulation is likely to play a significant role in the future of altcoins. While some altcoins may benefit from regulation, others may struggle to adapt to new regulatory frameworks. Additionally, regulatory uncertainty may lead to volatility in the altcoin market and hinder adoption and investment.

Competition The success of altcoins will also depend on competition from other cryptocurrencies and traditional payment methods. While altcoins offer unique value propositions, they will need to continue to innovate and improve to remain competitive. Additionally, traditional payment methods like credit cards and wire transfers may continue to dominate in certain use cases.

Network effects As with any network, the success of altcoins will depend on network effects. As more users adopt and use an altcoin, its value and utility will increase. However, network effects can also create a "winner takes all" scenario, where a single altcoin dominates the market and leaves little room for competitors.

Market trends Finally, the role of altcoins in the future of cryptocurrency will depend on broader market trends. As the crypto market evolves, it is possible that new use cases and applications for altcoins will emerge, driving demand and adoption. Conversely, the market may shift towards other forms of digital assets or decentralized finance, reducing the role of altcoins.

Overall, the role of altcoins in the future of cryptocurrency remains uncertain. However, their unique value propositions and potential for innovation make them an important component of the crypto ecosystem. Adoption, integration, competition, regulation, network effects, and market trends are likely to play important roles in determining the success of altcoins in the years to come.

Chapter 5: Altcoins Today
Overview of the current state of altcoins

The cryptocurrency market has evolved significantly since the introduction of Bitcoin in 2009, with a plethora of alternative cryptocurrencies (altcoins) now available. Altcoins have gained in popularity over the years and are now an essential part of the broader cryptocurrency ecosystem. This chapter will provide an overview of the current state of altcoins, including their adoption, market capitalization, and recent developments.

Adoption of altcoins

Altcoins have gained widespread adoption, with many crypto investors diversifying their portfolios to include these alternative cryptocurrencies. While Bitcoin remains the most dominant cryptocurrency by market capitalization, altcoins have made significant inroads in recent years. Altcoins are now used for a wide range of purposes, from decentralized finance (DeFi) to non-fungible tokens (NFTs) and smart contracts.

Market capitalization

The market capitalization of altcoins has grown significantly over the years. According to CoinMarketCap, the total market capitalization of altcoins was around $1.1 trillion as of September 2021, with Bitcoin accounting for around 40% of the total market capitalization. Ethereum, the second-largest cryptocurrency by market capitalization, accounts for around 18% of the total market capitalization. Other altcoins such as Binance Coin, Cardano, and Dogecoin have also seen significant growth in market capitalization in recent years.

Recent developments

Altcoins continue to evolve, with new cryptocurrencies being introduced regularly. Many of these new cryptocurrencies are designed to address specific challenges or provide unique features that existing cryptocurrencies do not offer. For example, Solana is a high-performance blockchain designed to provide fast and scalable transactions, while Avalanche is a platform that supports interoperability between different blockchains.

In addition to the introduction of new altcoins, there have been several significant developments in the altcoin space in recent years. For example, the rise of decentralized finance (DeFi) has led to the emergence of new altcoins that are designed specifically for use in DeFi protocols. Similarly, the rise of non-fungible tokens (NFTs) has led to the emergence of new altcoins designed to support NFT transactions.

Conclusion

Altcoins have come a long way since the introduction of Bitcoin in 2009. Today, altcoins are an essential part of the broader cryptocurrency ecosystem, with many investors diversifying their portfolios to include these alternative cryptocurrencies. The market capitalization of altcoins has grown significantly over the years, and there have been several significant developments in the altcoin space in recent years. As the cryptocurrency market continues to evolve, it is likely that altcoins will continue to play an important role in the future of cryptocurrency.

Examination of significant altcoins today

Altcoins, or alternative cryptocurrencies to Bitcoin, have come a long way since their inception in 2011. While Bitcoin remains the largest and most well-known cryptocurrency, altcoins have become increasingly popular and widespread. Today, there are over 8,000 altcoins available on various cryptocurrency exchanges, with a combined market capitalization of over $1 trillion.

Ethereum (ETH):

Ethereum is the second-largest cryptocurrency by market capitalization after Bitcoin. It was created in 2014 by Vitalik Buterin and has since grown to become the leading platform for decentralized applications (dApps) and smart contracts. Ethereum's blockchain allows developers to create their own tokens, which has resulted in the creation of many new altcoins. Additionally, Ethereum is currently undergoing a major upgrade known as Ethereum 2.0, which is expected to improve scalability and security.

Binance Coin (BNB):

Binance Coin is the native token of the Binance cryptocurrency exchange, which is one of the largest exchanges in the world. BNB is used to pay for transaction fees on the Binance platform, as well as for other services offered by the exchange. Binance also offers discounts on transaction fees for users who hold BNB, which has contributed to its popularity.

Cardano (ADA):

Cardano is a third-generation blockchain platform that was created by IOHK, a blockchain research and development firm led by Charles Hoskinson. Cardano aims to address some of the scalability and security issues that other blockchains, such as Ethereum, have faced. Cardano's native token, ADA, is used to pay for transaction fees and to participate in the platform's proof-of-stake consensus mechanism.

Dogecoin (DOGE):

Dogecoin was created in 2013 as a joke based on the popular "Doge" internet meme. However, it has since become a popular altcoin in its own right, with a market capitalization of over $8 billion. Dogecoin's popularity is largely driven by social media hype and celebrity endorsements, such as from Tesla CEO Elon Musk.

Polkadot (DOT):

Polkadot is a multi-chain platform that allows different blockchains to communicate with each other. It was created by Gavin Wood, who was also a co-founder of Ethereum. Polkadot's native token, DOT, is used to pay for transaction fees and to participate in the platform's governance system.

Solana (SOL):

Solana is a blockchain platform that was created in 2017 and has gained popularity due to its fast transaction processing times and low fees. Solana's blockchain can currently process over 50,000 transactions per second, which is significantly faster than other blockchains like Ethereum. Solana's native token, SOL, is used to pay for transaction fees and to participate in the platform's proof-of-stake consensus mechanism.

Ripple (XRP):

Ripple is a blockchain-based payment protocol that was created in 2012. Ripple's technology allows for fast and inexpensive cross-border payments, which has made it popular with banks and financial institutions. Ripple's native token, XRP, is used to facilitate transactions on the Ripple network.

Conclusion:

Altcoins have come a long way since their early days as Bitcoin clones. Today, there are thousands of altcoins available, each with their own unique features and use cases. While not all altcoins will succeed, the ones that do have the potential to revoluticnize industries and change the way we interact with money. As the cryptocurrency ecosystem continues to evolve, it will be interesting to see how altcoins continue to grow and impact the broader financial landscape.

Analysis of the impact of altcoins on the crypto industry

Altcoins have had a significant impact on the crypto industry since their emergence. As they continue to evolve and gain popularity, their impact on the industry is only expected to increase. In this section, we will examine the impact of altcoins on the crypto industry.

Competition for Bitcoin Altcoins have created competition for Bitcoin, the first and most well-known cryptocurrency. As altcoins have gained in popularity and utility, investors and traders have started to diversify their portfolios, leading to increased competition for Bitcoin. This competition has forced Bitcoin to improve its technology and functionality to remain relevant in the market.

Increased Adoption of Cryptocurrency The emergence of altcoins has increased the adoption of cryptocurrency by the general public. The increased competition among cryptocurrencies has resulted in a wider range of options for investors and traders, which has made it easier for people to invest in and use cryptocurrency. This increased adoption has brought more attention to the crypto industry and has helped to increase its legitimacy.

Innovation and Experimentation Altcoins have also been a driving force behind innovation and experimentation in the crypto industry. Many altcoins have introduced new features and technologies that have been adopted by other cryptocurrencies or have led to the development of entirely new cryptocurrencies. This experimentation has helped to drive the evolution of the industry and has led to the creation of new use cases and applications for cryptocurrency.

Volatility and Risk While the impact of altcoins on the crypto industry has been largely positive, their high volatility and risk have also had an impact. Altcoins are often subject to extreme price swings, which can make them attractive to traders but can also lead to significant losses. This volatility has led to increased scrutiny and regulation of the industry, as governments and financial institutions have sought to protect consumers from the risks associated with cryptocurrency.

Influence on Traditional Finance Finally, altcoins have also had an impact on traditional finance. As cryptocurrencies have gained popularity and acceptance, traditional financial institutions have started to take notice. Many have begun to explore the use of blockchain technology and cryptocurrencies in their operations, while others have introduced their own cryptocurrencies or have partnered with existing cryptocurrencies. This integration of cryptocurrencies and traditional finance is expected to continue and could lead to significant changes in the financial industry.

Overall, the impact of altcoins on the crypto industry has been significant and varied. While their high volatility and risk have led to increased scrutiny and regulation, their competition with Bitcoin, increased adoption, innovation and experimentation, and influence on traditional finance have helped to drive the evolution of the industry and have made it more accessible to a wider range of people. As the industry continues to evolve and new altcoins emerge, their impact on the industry is only expected to increase.

Exploration of the future of altcoins

As the crypto industry continues to evolve, the future of altcoins remains a topic of interest and speculation. There are many factors that could influence the direction of altcoins in the coming years, including regulation, adoption, technological advancements, and market trends.

One possibility is that altcoins will continue to grow in popularity and market share, challenging Bitcoin's dominance. Some altcoins are already establishing themselves as serious contenders to Bitcoin, such as Ethereum, Binance Coin, and Cardano. These altcoins have unique features and use cases that set them apart from Bitcoin and make them attractive to investors and developers alike.

Another potential future for altcoins is consolidation, where many of the less viable altcoins will fall by the wayside as the market becomes more crowded and competitive. This could lead to a smaller number of more established and valuable altcoins dominating the market.

Regulation will also play a significant role in the future of altcoins. Governments around the world are beginning to take notice of the crypto industry and are starting to regulate it more closely. This could have both positive and negative effects on altcoins, depending on the type of regulation introduced. While regulation could provide legitimacy and security to the industry, it could also stifle innovation and limit the growth of altcoins.

Adoption will also be a key factor in the future of altcoins. As more people become aware of cryptocurrencies and their potential, adoption rates could skyrocket, leading to increased demand for altcoins. However, mass adoption is still a long way off, and altcoins will need to continue to address issues such as usability, security, and scalability if they are to become widely used.

Technological advancements will also play a significant role in the future of altcoins. The development of new technologies such as blockchain interoperability, layer 2 scaling solutions, and decentralized finance (DeFi) could create new use cases and opportunities for altcoins.

Finally, market trends will continue to shape the future of altcoins. The crypto industry is known for its volatility, and altcoins are no exception. As the market continues to mature, altcoins will need to navigate fluctuations in price, market sentiment, and investor interest.

Overall, the future of altcoins is uncertain, but there is no doubt that they will continue to play an important role in the crypto industry. As the industry continues to evolve, altcoins will need to adapt and innovate to stay relevant and attractive to investors and users alike. Whether they will challenge Bitcoin's dominance or continue to carve out their own niche remains to be seen, but one thing is certain: the future of altcoins is full of potential and possibility.

Chapter 6: Altcoins vs Bitcoin

Comparison of altcoins and Bitcoin

Bitcoin, the first cryptocurrency, paved the way for a new era of digital assets. Over time, many other cryptocurrencies have emerged in the market, also known as altcoins. Altcoins are alternatives to Bitcoin, offering different features, use cases, and benefits. While both Bitcoin and altcoins are based on the same blockchain technology, they differ in several ways. In this chapter, we will compare altcoins and Bitcoin in terms of their features, use cases, and market performance.

Features:

Bitcoin and altcoins differ in their features, including the technology used, mining mechanisms, and transaction speed. Bitcoin uses the Proof of Work (PoW) consensus algorithm, while many altcoins use different consensus algorithms like Proof of Stake (PoS) and Delegated Proof of Stake (DPoS). PoW requires miners to solve complex mathematical equations to validate transactions and create new blocks, whereas PoS and DPoS rely on the amount of cryptocurrency held by the user as a stake.

Altcoins also offer different transaction speeds than Bitcoin. For instance, Ripple (XRP) can process up to 1,500 transactions per second, while Bitcoin can only handle up to

7 transactions per second. This means that XRP is faster and more efficient for payments and settlements.

Use Cases:

Bitcoin and altcoins have different use cases. Bitcoin was initially created as a decentralized digital currency to facilitate peer-to-peer transactions without the need for intermediaries. However, over time, Bitcoin has also become a store of value and a hedge against inflation, like gold.

On the other hand, altcoins offer different use cases, such as smart contracts, decentralized applications (DApps), privacy-focused transactions, and gaming. For example, Ethereum (ETH) was created as a platform for DApps and smart contracts. DApps built on Ethereum can execute self-executing code, automated transactions, and decentralized governance.

Market Performance:

Bitcoin and altcoins also differ in their market performance. Bitcoin is the most dominant cryptocurrency in terms of market capitalization, accounting for over 40% of the total crypto market cap. Altcoins, on the other hand, account for the remaining 60%, with some altcoins having a larger market share than others.

The market performance of altcoins is also more volatile than Bitcoin. Altcoins can experience significant price fluctuations due to market sentiment, adoption rates, and technological advancements. For example, altcoins like Dogecoin (DOGE) and Shiba Inu (SHIB) saw massive price surges in 2021 due to hype and social media attention.

Conclusion:

In conclusion, while Bitcoin and altcoins are based on the same blockchain technology, they differ in their features, use cases, and market performance. Altcoins offer different use cases, like smart contracts, privacy-focused transactions, and gaming, and have different consensus mechanisms and transaction speeds. Altcoins also have more volatile market performance than Bitcoin, which is often viewed as a safe haven asset. Overall, both Bitcoin and altcoins have their strengths and weaknesses, and it's up to investors to decide which assets suit their investment goals and risk tolerance.

Advantages and disadvantages of each

Introduction: The debate over which is better, Bitcoin or altcoins, is one that has been ongoing since the inception of altcoins. Both Bitcoin and altcoins have their advantages and disadvantages. In this section, we will explore the advantages and disadvantages of both Bitcoin and altcoins and compare the two.

Advantages of Bitcoin:

First mover advantage: Bitcoin was the first cryptocurrency, and this gives it a significant advantage. It is the most widely known and has the highest market capitalization.

Brand recognition: Bitcoin has become a household name, and many people are familiar with it, even if they don't know much about cryptocurrency. This brand recognition gives Bitcoin an advantage over other cryptocurrencies.

Stability: Bitcoin has been around for over a decade, and this has given it a level of stability that is lacking in many altcoins.

Decentralization: Bitcoin is a decentralized currency, which means that it is not controlled by any central authority. This decentralization makes Bitcoin more secure and resistant to censorship.

Disadvantages of Bitcoin:

Scalability: One of the biggest disadvantages of Bitcoin is its scalability problem. The network can only handle a limited number of transactions per second, which makes it slow and expensive to use.

Lack of innovation: Bitcoin has been around for over a decade, and while it is still the most popular cryptocurrency, it has not seen much innovation in recent years.

Environmental impact: Bitcoin mining requires a significant amount of energy, and this has a negative impact on the environment.

Advantages of Altcoins:

Innovation: Altcoins are often created to solve specific problems that Bitcoin cannot. This innovation has led to the creation of many interesting and useful cryptocurrencies.

Scalability: Many altcoins are designed to be more scalable than Bitcoin, which means they can handle a larger number of transactions per second.

Lower fees: Many altcoins have lower transaction fees than Bitcoin, making them more affordable to use.

Specialized use cases: Some altcoins are designed for specific use cases, such as privacy-focused coins or stablecoins.

Disadvantages of Altcoins:

Lack of brand recognition: Altcoins do not have the same brand recognition as Bitcoin, which can make them harder to use and harder to sell.

Risky investments: Many altcoins are very volatile and can be risky investments.

Security concerns: Altcoins are often less secure than Bitcoin, which makes them more vulnerable to hacking and other security breaches.

Conclusion: Both Bitcoin and altcoins have their advantages and disadvantages. Bitcoin has the advantage of being the first cryptocurrency and having the most brand recognition, but it also has scalability issues and a lack of innovation. Altcoins offer innovation, scalability, and lower fees, but they also come with risks, such as lack of brand recognition and security concerns. Ultimately, the choice between Bitcoin and altcoins will depend on individual needs and preferences.

Examination of the relationship between altcoins and Bitcoin

Bitcoin was the first and original cryptocurrency, and it remains the most well-known and dominant in the market. However, altcoins have been introduced and have grown in popularity over the years, creating a diverse cryptocurrency ecosystem. While altcoins have their unique features and advantages, many are still tied to the value of Bitcoin. In this section, we will examine the relationship between altcoins and Bitcoin.

Altcoins and Bitcoin Market Correlation

The relationship between Bitcoin and altcoins is complex, but one of the most significant factors is their market correlation. The correlation between Bitcoin and altcoins can be positive, negative, or zero, and it can vary depending on market conditions.

In some cases, altcoins have shown a positive correlation with Bitcoin. This means that when the value of Bitcoin increases, the value of altcoins also increases. This is because investors see the growth of Bitcoin as a positive sign for the entire cryptocurrency market and, as a result, invest more heavily in altcoins. However, a positive correlation can also work in the opposite direction, with a decline in the value of Bitcoin resulting in a decline in the value of altcoins.

In other cases, altcoins have shown a negative correlation with Bitcoin. This means that when the value of Bitcoin increases, the value of altcoins decreases. This can happen when investors move their funds from altcoins to Bitcoin, either because they see Bitcoin as a safer investment or because they are trying to take advantage of Bitcoin's growth potential.

Finally, there can also be a zero correlation between Bitcoin and altcoins, which means that the two do not move in relation to each other. This can happen when the market is in a state of flux, and there is no clear trend in either direction.

Bitcoin Dominance and Altcoin Value

Another factor that can impact the relationship between Bitcoin and altcoins is Bitcoin dominance. Bitcoin dominance refers to the percentage of the total cryptocurrency market capitalization that is made up of Bitcoin. When Bitcoin dominance is high, it can have a negative impact on the value of altcoins because investors are more likely to put their money into Bitcoin rather than altcoins.

In contrast, when Bitcoin dominance is low, it can be positive for altcoins because investors are more likely to put their money into altcoins, which they see as having more growth potential. Altcoins can also offer unique features and advantages that Bitcoin does not have, such as faster transaction speeds or greater scalability.

Competition or Complementary?

There is ongoing debate in the cryptocurrency community about whether altcoins are in competition with Bitcoin or whether they are complementary to it. Some argue that altcoins are simply imitating Bitcoin and that they do not offer any real innovation or value. Others argue that altcoins can provide important features and benefits that Bitcoin cannot, such as faster transaction times or greater privacy.

One way to look at the relationship between Bitcoin and altcoins is to view them as complementary rather than in competition. Bitcoin serves as a store of value and a means of payment, while altcoins can offer additional functionality and features that can complement Bitcoin's strengths. For example, while Bitcoin is the dominant cryptocurrency for store of value, privacy coins such as Monero and Zcash offer a greater degree of anonymity and security.

Conclusion

Altcoins and Bitcoin have a complex and evolving relationship. While altcoins have their unique features and advantages, they are still often tied to the value of Bitcoin.

Understanding the relationship between Bitcoin and altcoins is essential for investors looking to navigate the cryptocurrency market. Additionally, recognizing the complementary relationship between Bitcoin and altcoins can help investors to take advantage of the unique features and benefits offered by both. Ultimately, the future of altcoins and Bitcoin will depend on market conditions, technological advancements, and the ongoing evolution of the cryptocurrency ecosystem.

Analysis of the potential future impact of altcoins and Bitcoin

Altcoins and Bitcoin have already made a significant impact on the financial world, and it is clear that they will continue to do so in the future. Both have unique advantages and disadvantages, and the competition between them is fierce. While Bitcoin is the oldest and most well-known cryptocurrency, altcoins are growing in popularity and influence. In this section, we will explore the potential future impact of both altcoins and Bitcoin.

Bitcoin's Impact

Bitcoin has already had a significant impact on the financial world. It has disrupted traditional banking and financial institutions by allowing individuals to conduct transactions directly without the need for a third party. Its decentralization and lack of government control have made it an attractive alternative for people around the world.

a. Potential Impact on Traditional Banking

Bitcoin's impact on traditional banking has already been significant. It has provided an alternative to the traditional banking system, which many people find more accessible and convenient. In the future, as more people adopt Bitcoin, it could lead to a further decline in traditional banking, which could have significant economic consequences.

b. Potential Impact on Government Control

Bitcoin's decentralization has made it an attractive alternative for people who want to avoid government control. In countries where governments restrict access to financial services, Bitcoin has provided an alternative means of conducting transactions. However, as Bitcoin continues to grow in popularity, governments may seek to regulate it more closely. This could have a significant impact on the future of Bitcoin.

c. Potential Impact on International Trade

Bitcoin has the potential to revolutionize international trade by making it easier and more efficient. Bitcoin's lack of intermediaries means that transactions can be conducted more quickly and at a lower cost than traditional methods. In the future, as more businesses adopt Bitcoin, it could become a standard means of conducting international trade.

Altcoins' Impact

Altcoins are still a relatively new concept, but they have already had an impact on the crypto industry. They offer unique advantages over Bitcoin, such as faster transaction times, lower fees, and more privacy. In the future, they could play an even more significant role in the financial world.

a. Potential Impact on Bitcoin

Altcoins could have a significant impact on Bitcoin. As more altcoins are developed and gain popularity, they could potentially steal market share from Bitcoin. Altcoins with unique features could attract users away from Bitcoin, which could cause Bitcoin's value to decline.

b. Potential Impact on Traditional Banking

Altcoins could have a significant impact on traditional banking. As more people adopt altcoins, they could potentially shift away from traditional banking. This could lead to a decline in traditional banking, which could have significant economic consequences.

c. Potential Impact on Government Control

Altcoins have the potential to provide even more privacy and decentralization than Bitcoin. As more people adopt altcoins, they could potentially avoid government control even more effectively than with Bitcoin. This could lead to further government regulations and restrictions on altcoins.

Future Impact of Altcoins and Bitcoin

The future impact of altcoins and Bitcoin is still uncertain. However, it is clear that they will continue to play a significant role in the financial world. In the future, we could see even more innovative altcoins that offer unique features and advantages over Bitcoin. Additionally, Bitcoin could continue to grow in popularity and become even more widely accepted as a means of payment.

a. Potential for Coexistence

It is possible that both altcoins and Bitcoin will continue to coexist in the future. Bitcoin's strong brand recognition and wide acceptance make it an attractive option for many people, while altcoins offer unique features and advantages that Bitcoin does not.

b. Potential for Dominance

Bitcoin has maintained its dominance over the cryptocurrency market since its creation, but there are several altcoins that have gained significant market share in recent years. The potential for dominance by altcoins is a topic of much debate among cryptocurrency enthusiasts.

One factor to consider is the utility of the altcoin. Altcoins with specific use cases that are not covered by Bitcoin may gain more traction in their respective industries. For example, Ethereum is known for its smart contract functionality, which has allowed for the creation of decentralized applications (dApps) that can execute automatically based on pre-determined conditions. This unique feature has led to the development of an entire ecosystem of projects and applications built on the Ethereum blockchain. Other altcoins, such as Litecoin and Bitcoin Cash, have focused on increasing transaction speeds and lowering fees, making them more attractive for day-to-day transactions.

Another factor to consider is the level of adoption and acceptance by businesses and individuals. Bitcoin has gained widespread recognition and acceptance, with many large companies now accepting Bitcoin payments. However, there are also a growing number of businesses that accept other cryptocurrencies, including altcoins. For example, in 2021, Tesla announced that it would accept Bitcoin as payment for its electric vehicles, but it also stated that it would consider other cryptocurrencies in the future.

Additionally, the development of decentralized finance (DeFi) has given rise to new opportunities for altcoins to gain dominance. DeFi refers to a range of financial services and applications built on decentralized blockchain networks. These networks often use their own native tokens for transaction fees and governance, giving rise to the potential for altcoins to play a significant role in the DeFi ecosystem.

Despite these opportunities, it is important to note that Bitcoin still holds a significant advantage in terms of network effects and brand recognition. The Bitcoin network has been operating for over a decade and has a large and dedicated user base. This gives it an advantage over newer altcoins that may struggle to gain the same level of recognition and adoption.

Another potential barrier for altcoins is regulatory uncertainty. Governments around the world are still grappling with how to regulate cryptocurrencies, and this uncertainty can make it difficult for altcoins to gain widespread adoption. Some countries have outright banned the use of cryptocurrencies, while others have implemented strict regulations that make it difficult for businesses to operate in the industry.

In summary, while there are opportunities for altcoins to gain dominance in the cryptocurrency market, there are also significant barriers to overcome. The utility of the altcoin, level of adoption and acceptance, development of DeFi, network effects, brand recognition, and regulatory uncertainty are all factors that will play a role in determining which cryptocurrencies will dominate the market in the future.

Conclusion

Recap of the impact of altcoins on the crypto industry

As we conclude this comprehensive analysis of altcoins, it is essential to recap the impact they have had on the cryptocurrency industry as a whole. Altcoins have transformed the cryptocurrency landscape by offering a new range of use cases and applications that Bitcoin could not achieve. In addition, they have introduced new technologies and features that have been instrumental in advancing the blockchain ecosystem.

One of the most significant impacts of altcoins is that they have spurred healthy competition in the cryptocurrency market. The presence of multiple cryptocurrencies means that users have more choices, and developers are continuously pushing the boundaries to offer better and more innovative solutions. This competition has resulted in a more diverse cryptocurrency market, which, in turn, has helped to enhance its credibility and longevity.

Furthermore, altcoins have played an instrumental role in the development of decentralized finance (DeFi) applications. Many altcoins have introduced smart contract functionality, which has enabled developers to build sophisticated financial applications on the blockchain. DeFi has revolutionized the traditional finance industry by offering a decentralized alternative to traditional financial institutions and services.

The rise and fall of altcoins have also provided valuable lessons to the cryptocurrency industry. The success of altcoins such as Ethereum and Litecoin has demonstrated that cryptocurrencies can serve different purposes and that their potential applications are vast. However, the failures of other altcoins have highlighted the importance of robust governance, security, and sustainability. These lessons have been instrumental in shaping the development and adoption of cryptocurrencies, particularly for new projects entering the market.

Another crucial impact of altcoins is that they have introduced new concepts and technologies to the cryptocurrency industry. Some of the notable examples include proof-of-stake (PoS) consensus algorithms, sharding, and interoperability solutions. These technologies have helped to address some of the scalability and interoperability challenges that Bitcoin faces and have provided the industry with new and innovative solutions.

Finally, altcoins have had an impact on the overall adoption and mainstream recognition of cryptocurrencies. While Bitcoin is still the most recognizable and widely adopted cryptocurrency, the presence of altcoins has helped to increase overall awareness and understanding of cryptocurrencies. This has helped to drive broader adoption, particularly in regions where cryptocurrencies were previously unknown or untested.

In conclusion, the impact of altcoins on the cryptocurrency industry has been significant and far-reaching. They have introduced new use cases, technologies, and concepts that have helped to transform the industry. Altcoins have also played a critical role in spurring competition, promoting innovation, and enhancing the overall adoption and mainstream recognition of cryptocurrencies. As the industry continues to evolve, it is likely that altcoins will continue to play a critical role in driving its growth and success.

Reflection on the lessons learned from the rise and fall of altcoins

Throughout the history of the cryptocurrency industry, altcoins have played a significant role in shaping the market and driving innovation. While some altcoins have been successful and have become prominent players in the industry, many have failed to gain traction and ultimately collapsed. As we conclude this discussion on the evolution of altcoins, it is important to reflect on the lessons learned from their rise and fall.

One of the most important lessons learned from the rise and fall of altcoins is the importance of innovation and differentiation. Many of the altcoins that failed were simply trying to replicate the success of Bitcoin without offering anything new or unique. On the other hand, altcoins that were successful differentiated themselves by offering innovative features and capabilities that Bitcoin could not match. This highlights the importance of continuous innovation in the cryptocurrency industry, and the need to constantly push the boundaries of what is possible.

Another lesson learned is the importance of community and adoption. Successful altcoins not only offered innovative features, but also built strong communities around their projects. These communities provided the necessary support and momentum for the altcoins to gain traction and achieve widespread adoption. Conversely, altcoins that failed often lacked a strong community and struggled to gain traction as a result. This highlights the importance of building a strong and engaged community around a cryptocurrency project to ensure its success.

A third lesson learned is the importance of transparency and trust. Cryptocurrencies, including altcoins, have faced challenges in gaining widespread adoption due to their association with illegal activities and lack of regulation. Successful altcoins have been able to build trust with users and the broader public by being transparent about their operations and complying with relevant regulations. This has helped to increase confidence in the legitimacy of these altcoins, and has contributed to their long-term success.

Finally, the rise and fall of altcoins has also highlighted the importance of diversification in the cryptocurrency industry. While Bitcoin remains the dominant cryptocurrency, the rise of altcoins has provided users with a greater range of options and has contributed to the overall growth and development of the industry. The future success of the cryptocurrency industry is likely to depend on the continued development of a diverse range of altcoins, each with their own unique features and capabilities.

In conclusion, the evolution of altcoins has been a significant part of the cryptocurrency industry and has contributed to its growth and development. While many altcoins have failed, the lessons learned from their rise and fall have helped to shape the industry and provide insights into the keys to success. As the industry continues to evolve, it will be important to remember these lessons and to continue to innovate and differentiate in order to ensure the long-term success of cryptocurrency projects.

Examination of the potential future of altcoins

The future of altcoins is a topic of great interest to many in the cryptocurrency community. While some believe that altcoins will continue to play a major role in the crypto industry, others argue that they may eventually be overtaken by Bitcoin or other dominant cryptocurrencies.

One potential future for altcoins is continued growth and adoption. As discussed earlier, many altcoins have unique features and use cases that distinguish them from Bitcoin and other cryptocurrencies. As more people become aware of these features and begin to use altcoins for specific purposes, demand for these coins could continue to increase. Additionally, as blockchain technology continues to evolve, new use cases for altcoins may emerge, further driving adoption and growth.

However, there are also several factors that could limit the future potential of altcoins. One of the biggest challenges facing altcoins is competition from Bitcoin. As the dominant cryptocurrency, Bitcoin has significant network effects and is often the first choice for investors and traders. This could make it difficult for altcoins to gain a foothold in the market and establish themselves as viable alternatives.

Another challenge facing altcoins is regulatory uncertainty. As governments around the world continue to grapple with the rise of cryptocurrencies, there is a risk that increased regulation could stifle innovation and limit the growth of altcoins. This could make it difficult for altcoins to gain mainstream adoption and compete with more established cryptocurrencies like Bitcoin.

Despite these challenges, many in the cryptocurrency community remain optimistic about the future of altcoins. Some believe that the continued development of blockchain technology will create new opportunities for altcoins, while others point to the growing popularity of decentralized finance (DeFi) as evidence of the potential for altcoins to play a major role in the crypto ecosystem.

In particular, DeFi platforms are built on top of blockchain technology and allow users to access a wide range of financial services without the need for intermediaries. Many of these platforms are built using Ethereum and other altcoins, and the growth of DeFi could drive increased demand for these coins.

Another potential future for altcoins is increased collaboration and interoperability. As the cryptocurrency industry matures, it is becoming increasingly clear that different cryptocurrencies have different strengths and weaknesses. Rather than competing against each other, many in the community believe that altcoins should work together to create a more robust and resilient ecosystem. This could involve increased collaboration between different blockchain platforms, as well as the development of interoperability protocols that allow different cryptocurrencies to work together seamlessly.

In conclusion, the potential future of altcoins is uncertain, but there are several factors that could determine their success or failure. While competition from Bitcoin and regulatory uncertainty are significant challenges, the continued growth of blockchain technology and the rise of DeFi could create new opportunities for altcoins to thrive. Additionally, increased collaboration and interoperability between different cryptocurrencies could help to create a more robust and resilient crypto ecosystem. Ultimately, the future of altcoins will depend on a wide range of factors, including technological innovation, market demand, and regulatory developments.

Final thoughts on the role of altcoins in the future of cryptocurrency

As we've seen throughout this book, altcoins have played a significant role in the development of the cryptocurrency industry. From their early beginnings as simple Bitcoin clones to the emergence of new, innovative projects with unique features and capabilities, altcoins have helped to push the boundaries of what's possible in the world of digital assets.

But as we've also seen, altcoins have faced their fair share of challenges, from technical issues to market volatility to outright fraud and scams. These challenges have led many to question the long-term viability of altcoins and their place in the broader cryptocurrency ecosystem.

So what does the future hold for altcoins? Will they continue to play an important role in the development of cryptocurrency, or will they ultimately be overshadowed by Bitcoin and other dominant players?

One thing is clear: altcoins are not going away anytime soon. Despite their challenges, there are still thousands of altcoins in circulation, with new projects launching all the time. Many of these projects are working to solve real-world problems and address unmet needs in the market, which suggests that there will always be a place for altcoins in the cryptocurrency ecosystem.

At the same time, it's important to acknowledge that not all altcoins will be successful. The market is highly competitive, and many projects will struggle to gain traction and achieve widespread adoption. Some will fail outright, while others may limp along with only a small community of supporters.

Ultimately, the success of any altcoin project will depend on a variety of factors, including its technical capabilities, its user base, its governance structure, and its ability to compete with other projects in the market.

One potential area where altcoins could thrive is in providing specialized use cases or applications that are not well-suited for Bitcoin or other dominant cryptocurrencies. For example, some altcoins may focus on privacy and security, while others may be designed specifically for use in certain industries or geographic regions.

At the same time, it's important to recognize that altcoins will never be able to completely replace Bitcoin as the dominant player in the cryptocurrency market. Bitcoin's first-mover advantage, brand recognition, and network effects give it a level of dominance that is difficult to match.

That said, altcoins may still play an important role in diversifying the cryptocurrency ecosystem and providing users with more options and opportunities. As the industry continues to evolve and mature, it will be interesting to see how altcoins continue to adapt and grow, and what new innovations they bring to the table.

In the end, the future of altcoins is uncertain, but one thing is clear: they have already made a significant impact on the cryptocurrency industry and will likely continue to do so for years to come. Whether they ultimately succeed or fail, altcoins represent an important chapter in the history of cryptocurrency, and their legacy will continue to be felt for many years to come.

THE END

Potential References

Introduction:

Antonopoulos, A. M. (2014). Mastering Bitcoin: Unlocking Digital Cryptocurrencies. O'Reilly Media, Inc.

Buterin, V. (2014). A next-generation smart contract and decentralized application platform. White Paper, Ethereum Project, 1-32.

Nakamoto, S. (2008). Bitcoin: A peer-to-peer electronic cash system.

Chapter 1: The Pioneers

Popper, N. (2016). Digital Gold: Bitcoin and the Inside Story of the Misfits and Millionaires Trying to Reinvent Money. HarperCollins.

Srinivasan, B. (2014). Bitcoin 2.0: Sidechains and Ethereum. O'Reilly Radar.

Chapter 2: The Rise of Altcoins

Lee, C. (2011). Litecoin: Open source P2P digital currency. GitHub. Retrieved from https://github.com/litecoin-project/litecoin/blob/master/doc/litecoin-whitepaper.pdf.

Swan, M. (2015). Blockchain: blueprint for a new economy. O'Reilly Media, Inc.

Chapter 3: The Fall of Altcoins

Diakun, A. (2018). The 10 worst cryptocurrencies by losses. Retrieved from https://www.cryptopolitan.com/10-worst-cryptocurrencies-by-losses/.

Fisch, B., & Böhme, R. (2015). On the intrinsic value of bitcoin: Evidence from mining difficulty data. Available at SSRN 2649770.

Chapter 4: The Evolution of Altcoins

Zohar, A. (2015). Bitcoin: under the hood. Communications of the ACM, 58(9), 104-113.

Casey, M. J., & Vigna, P. (2018). The truth machine: The blockchain and the future of everything. St. Martin's Press.

Chapter 5: Altcoins Today

CoinMarketCap. (2023). Cryptocurrency market capitalizations. Retrieved from https://coinmarketcap.com/.

Hoskinson, C., & Wood, G. (2014). The Ethereum white paper. Retrieved from https://ethereum.org/en/whitepaper/.

Chapter 6: Altcoins vs Bitcoin

Wattenhofer, R. (2015). Decentralized trusted timestamps in the bitcoin blockchain. In Proceedings of the 2015 ACM Conference on Special Interest Group on Data Communication (pp. 185-198).

Antonopoulos, A. M. (2018). Mastering Ethereum: Building Smart Contracts and DApps. O'Reilly Media, Inc.

Conclusion:

Chuen, D. L. K., & Nadarajah, S. (2015). Bitcoin and Cryptocurrency Technologies: A Comprehensive Introduction. Princeton University Press.

Narayanan, A., Bonneau, J., Felten, E., Miller, A., & Goldfeder, S. (2016). Bitcoin and Cryptocurrency Technologies: A Comprehensive Introduction. Princeton University Press.